165

Valentine's Day Jokes

What did one flame say to the other on Valentine's Day?

We're a perfect match!

What did one magnet say to the other?

I find you very attractive.

What happened to your leg?

I went to a seafood dance on Valentine's Day and pulled a mussel!

What do pigs give out on February 14th?

Valen-swines

What did the boy mouth freshener say to the girl mouth freshener?

We're mint for each other.

Why do melons have to get married in a church?

So that they cantaloupe!

Two antennae fell in love and got married. Their wedding was okay. The reception though was excellent.

What did the Valentine's Day card say to the stamp?

Stick with me and you'll go places!

Once upon a time a man was walking through the woods when he came upon an old gnome.

The old gnome warned him about dangerous purple mushrooms in the forest.

"If you accidentally step on one of the purple mushrooms, you will be forced to marry the ugliest person in the world!"

So the man carefully went through the forest making sure not to step on any of the mushrooms.

When he got to the end, a beautiful woman suddenly appeared and said "We have to marry."

The man replied smiling "Why?"

"Because I stepped on one of those purple mushrooms!" she replied.

A woman woke up from her dream and explained to her husband that he had bought her a beautiful diamond necklace for Valentine's Day.

She asked him what it meant. He replied saying that she would know by tonight.

After work, her husband came back with a small package for her. Delighted, she opened it and found a book called "The Meaning of Dreams".

Why do oars fall in love?

Because they're row-mantic.

Why can't you be my Valentine?

For medical reasons. You make me sick!

What do farmers give their wives on Valentine's Day?

Hogs and kisses

When you are with the right person, every day is like Valentine's Day. On the other hand, if every day feels like a funeral, run!

To all my friends who are in love, Happy Valentine's Day! To all my friends who are not, Happy Independence Day!

It's Valentine's Day so if you're secretly in love with me, then now would be the absolute perfect time to reveal it!

That moment when Valentine's Day is around the corner and you see that no one loves you like Mom does!

To all the people out there who don't celebrate Valentine's, don't be sad. Think of all the time and money you are saving on not getting a gift!

Whale you be my Valentine?
Dolphinately

Who are you spending Valentine's Day with?
With my ex... box one.

Do you have a date for Valentine's Day?

Yes, February 14th.

What did the pencil say to the paper?

I dot my i's on you!

What did one oar say to the other?

May I interest you in some row-mance?

Why is Valentine's Day the best day for celebration?

Because you can party hearty!

What is the true purpose of Valentine's Day?

To remind you how important love is!

Why did the boy put clothes on the Valentine he was sending?

Because it needed to be ad-dressed.

What did the painter say to her boyfriend?

I love you with all my art!

What do people who don't celebrate Valentine's Day call it?

Happy Independence Day

What's the difference between you and a calendar?

A calendar has a date on Valentine's Day.

What's the best part about Valentine's Day?

All the chocolate on sale!

Why did the pig give her boyfriend a box of chocolates?

It was Valenswine's Day!

Do skunks celebrate Valentine's Day?

Yes, they're very scent-imental.

What is the acronym for Valentine's Day?
R.C.D. (Roses & Chocolates Day)

What did the man with the broken leg say to his nurse?
I've got a crutch on you!

What do you call 2 birds in love?

Tweethearts

Did you hear about the romance in the tropical fish tank?

It was a case of guppy love.

What do you call a really small Valentine?

Valentiny

What did the chocolate say to the ice cream?

You're sweet!

What did the paper clip say to the magnet?

I find you very attractive.

What did the French chef give his wife on Valentine's Day?

A hug and a quiche

What did one pickle say to the other?

You mean a great dill to me.

**Knock Knock
Who's there?
Olive.
Olive who?
Olive you!**

What did the elephant say to her boyfriend?

I love you a ton!

What did the bat say to his girlfriend?

I like to hang out with you.

What happened when the man fell in love with his garden?

He wed (wet) his plants (pants)!

Did you hear about the nearsighted porcupine?

He fell in love with a pincushion!

What did the bear say to his girlfriend on Valentine's Day?

I love you beary much!

Why should you never break up with a goalie?

Because they're keepers!

What did the thunder give her boyfriend on Valentine's Day?

A box of shockolates

Why did the Goddess of Love become a Blackjack dealer?

Because she was always great at the Cupid Shuffle.

Why did the man put his girlfriend in jail?

Because she stole his heart.

What did the ocean say to the chicken on Valentine's Day?

Nothing. It just waved.

What did the squirrel say to her boyfriend on Valentine's Day?

You drive me nuts!

How did the telephone propose to his girlfriend?

He gave her a ring.

What is a zombie's sweetheart called?

His ghoul-friend

What did the drum say to the other drum on Valentine's Day?

My heart beats for you.

What did the cavemen give their girlfriends on Valentine's Day?

Lots of ughhhs and kisses!

What did Steve say to his girlfriend? (Minecraft joke)

I dig you.

What did the calculator say to the pencil on Valentine's Day?

You can always count on me.

What did the bee say to his girlfriend on Valentine's Day?

You are bee-utiful!

What did the sheep say to her boyfriend on Valentine's Day?

You're not so baaaa-d.

What did Frankenstein say to his Valentine?

Will you be my Valenstein?

What did the slug say to his girlfriend on Valentine's Day?

Will you be my Valenslime?

What did the owl say to his mate on Valentine's?

Owl be yours forever.

What kind of flowers should you never give your girlfriend?

Cauliflowers

If your aunt ran away to get married, what would you call her?

Antelope

What kind of makeup do witches use on Valentine's Day?

Mas-scare-a

Why didn't the skeleton go to the prom?

He had no body to dance with.

What is a ram's favorite song on Valentine's Day?

I only have eyes for ewe my love.

What did the snake give his girlfriend on Valentine's Day?

A hug and a hiss

What did the octopus ask his wife on Valentine's Day?

May I hold your hand, hand, hand, hand, hand, hand, hand, and hand?

What did the cat say to her boyfriend on Valentine's Day?

You're purr-fect for me!

What did the light bulb say to the switch on Valentine's Day?

You light me up!

Why did the boy put candy under his pillow before going to sleep?

He wanted sweet dreams.

What happens when you fall in love with a chef?

You get buttered up.

Why did the banana go out with the prune?

Because he couldn't get a date.

What did the two volcanoes say to each other?

I lava you!

What's Cupid's favorite TV show?

Arrow

What's the most romantic part of a fork?

Its Valen-tines

How is lettuce the most loving vegetable?

Because it's got heart.

Knock knock
Who's there?
Luke
Luke who?
Luke who's got a
Valentine!

Knock knock
Who's there?
Sherwood
Sherwood who?
Sherwood like to be your Valentine!

What happened to the two angels who got married?

They lived harpily ever after.

What's the most romantic city in the UK?

Loverpool

What did the strawberry say to the blueberry on Valentine's Day?

I love you berry much!

Where did the hamburger take his girlfriend out to dance?

The meatball

What did the two lightbulbs say to each other on Valentine's Day?

I love you a watt!

Did Adam and Eve ever have a date?

No they had an apple!

Did you hear about the bed bugs who fell in love?

They're getting married in the spring.

Why should you never date a pastry chef?

Because they'll always dessert you!

What's the best Valentine's Day chocolate to give a girl?

Her-she kisses

How does Cupid make so much money at the casino?

Because he's a Valentine's card shark.

What did the fungi say to each other on Valentine's Day?

There is so mushroom for you in my heart!

What did the toast say to the butter on Valentine's Day?

You're my butter half.

What did the muffin say to her boyfriend on Valentine's Day?

You're my stud-muffin!

What did the watermelon say to the cantaloupe?

You're one in a melon!

Why did the coffee lover have trouble expressing himself on Valentine's Day?

Words couldn't espresso how much she meant to him.

Who did Sladar send flowers to?

His Slihereen Crush

What did the beet say to his girlfriend on Valentine's Day?

When I'm around you, my heart beets faster.

How did Chen know he was in love with Enchantress?

Because the further he got from her the more it hurt.

If you were a triangle, you'd be acute one.

What did the mushroom say to her boyfriend on Valentine's?

I like you because you're a fun-gi to be around.

Why did he give his girlfriend a cannoli on Valentine's Day?

I cannoli be happy when I'm with you.

I better buy spell immunity because you are stunnin'.

What's the difference between a $20 steak and a $55 steak?

February 14th.

Knock knock
Who's there?
Frank
Frank who?
Frank you for being my Valentine!

What is the difference between a girl who is sick of her boyfriend and a sailor who falls into the ocean?

One is bored over a man the other is a man overboard.

Knock knock
Who's there?
Emma
Emma who?
Emma hoping I get a lot of cards on Valentine's Day!

What did the rabbit say to his girlfriend on Valentine's Day?

Somebunny loves you!

What did the whale say to his girlfriend on Valentine's Day?

Whale you be mine?

Knock knock
Who's there?
Pooch
Pooch who?
Pooch your arms around me!

Knock knock
Who's there?
Atlas
Atlas who?
Atlas, it's finally Valentine's Day!

Why wasn't Clinkz at his prom?

He had nobody to go with.

Mario is red, Sonic is blue, press start to join and be my player 2!

A boyfriend asks his girlfriend:

"What gift would you like to receive on Valentine's Day?"

"Well, I don't know" she answers shyly.

"OK, I'll give you another year to think about it!"

I donated blood today. It may not be the best Valentine's Day present but at least it came from the heart.

My wife called me at work on Valentine's Day.

She said, "Three of the girls in the office have just received bunches of flowers. They're absolutely gorgeous."

I said, "That's probably why they've been sent flowers then!"

This year I've got my wife a Valentine's Day present that will really take her breath away... a treadmill.

Maybe it's not my fault that I'm alone on Valentine's Day... maybe Cupid is just a bad shot!

I got my wife a new iron for Valentine's Day... she was so overcome with emotion that she ran out of the house crying.

What travels around the world but stays in one corner?

A stamp

Where does your girlfriend work?

At the zoo. I think she's a keeper!

Why is Junkrat such a likeable guy? - Overwatch joke (OJ)

He has such an explosive personality.

Never laugh at your girlfriend's choices because you are one of them!

Why is Roadhog such a likeable guy? (OJ)

I don't know but I'm always hooked after talking to him.

Never laugh at your girlfriend's choices because you are one of them!

A wife asks her husband, "How would you describe me?"

He replies, "ABCDEFGHIJK."

The confused wife asks, "What does that mean?"

Her husband replies, "Adorable, beautiful, cute, delightful, elegant, fashionable, gorgeous, and humorous."

The wife says, "Aw, thank you, but what about IJK?"

"I'm just kidding!"

How did McCree do in the beauty pageant? (OJ)

He was stunning.

Does Torbjörn have a crush on Mei? (OJ)

Yeah but she keeps giving him the cold shoulder.

Have you ever been on Widowmaker's webpage? (OJ)

I heard it's impossible to escape her site.

Why do all the ladies love Winston? (OJ)

Because of his shocking personality.

Why is Mei so easy to talk to? (OJ)

She knows how to break the ice.

Why does Pharah have a crush on Roadhog? (OJ)

She was hooked at first sight.

Why can't hydralisks get girlfriends? (Starcraft Joke)

Because they turn into lurkers.

What happened when two vampires went out on a blind date?

It was love at first bite!

What do you get when you kiss a dragon on Valentine's Day?

Third degree burns

How does Cupid visit his girlfriend?

On his arrow-plane!

Who did Dracula take to the movies?

His ghoul-friend

Why did the chicken cross the road?

Because her boyfriend was on the other side.

What do bunnies do when they get married?

They go on a bunnymoon!

What did the dog say to his girlfriend on Valentine's Day?

I drool-y do love you!

What did the ghost say to his girlfriend?

You look boo-tiful.

Why did you send your Valentine through Twitter?

Because she is my tweetheart!

What flowers give the most kisses on Valentine's Day?

Tulips

Why did the Rooster dress up on Valentine's Day?

He wanted to impress all the chicks.

Knock Knock
Who's there?
Cheese
Cheese who?
Cheese a cute girl!

Knock Knock
Who's there?
Howard
Howard who?
Howard you like a big hug?

What kind of treat is never on time?
ChocoLATE

What did Pilgrims give each other on Valentine's Day?
Mayflowers

What food is crazy about Valentine's Day chocolate?

A cocoa-nut

Why didn't the skeleton want to send any Valentine's Day cards?

His heart wasn't in it!

What does a car lover do on Valentine's Day?

They give it a Valenshine!

Did you hear about the guy who promised his wife a diamond?

He took her to a baseball field!

What does a carpet salesman give his wife for Valentine's Day?

Rugs and kisses

What happened when the two tennis players met?

It was lob at first sight!

What did one piece of string say to the other on Valentine's Day?

Be my Valentwine.

What did one doorbell say to the other on Valentine's Day?

Be my Valenchime.

Happy Valentine's Day!

We hope you had lots of fun and laughs!

As a special thank you for purchasing this book, please enjoy this exclusive preview from one of our other best sellers.

HILARIOUS JOKES
FOR

YEAR OLD KIDS

What do you call a fake noodle?

An IMPASTA

Why did the banana go to the doctor's office?

He wasn't peeling very well!

What animals have to wear wigs?

BALD Eagles

What makes ghosts bad liars?

You can see right through 'em!

What's a cow with no legs called?

<u>Ground</u> beef

What do you call cheese that doesn't belong to you?

Na-cho cheese

Where do cows like to go to on the weekends?

The moooooovies

What is an alligator in a vest called?

An in<u>vesti</u><u>gator</u>

A Message From the Publisher

Hello! My name is Hayden and I am the owner of Hayden Fox Publishing, the publishing house that brought you this title.

My hope is that your little one loved this book and enjoyed each and every page. If they did, please think about leaving a review for us on Amazon or wherever you purchased this book. It may only take a moment, but it really does mean the world for small businesses like mine.

The mission of Hayden Fox Publishing is to create premium content for children and their families that will help kids learn new things, make them think, put smiles on their faces, spend more quality time with family and have tons of fun doing it! Without you, however, this would not be possible, so we sincerely thank you for your purchase and for supporting our company mission.

~ Hayden

Check out our other books!

For more, visit our Amazon store at:
amazon.com/author/haydenfox

Made in the USA
Monee, IL
06 February 2021